DEDICATION

To my parents, Sukye and Orlando Bullock, whose love, strength, and courage has given my brothers and I life; for without them, this story would not exist.

To every child (and inner "grown-up" child) around the world who fully embraces the beauty of being "different". This one's for all of you, from my heart to yours.

Love,

Jungmiwha

Text copyright © 2014 by Dr. Jungmiwha Bullock
Illustrations copyright © 2014 by Dr. Jungmiwha Bullock and Christopher Matthews

First Hardcover Edition
10 9 8 7 6 5 4 3 2 1
Library of Congress Cataloging-in-Publication Data on file
ISBN-13: 978-1-941567-00-5 (Hardcover) | ISBN-10: 1-941567-00-2

www.amihalfgiraffe.com

Summary: A proud little girl from a giraffe and lion family wishes to figure out which "half" is her true identity, until she learns something far more important at the end. A multilingual book written completely in five languages, one diverse story (English, French, Spanish, Korean, and Afrikaans).

Audience: Ages 4 and up
[1. Multilingualism. 2. Identity--Fiction. 3. Giraffes--Fiction. 4. Lions--Fiction. 5. Bullying--Juvenile Fiction. 6. Racially mixed people--Fiction.
7. French language materials--Juvenile literature. 8. Spanish language materials--Juvenile literature. 9. Korean language materials--Juvenile literature.
10. Afrikaans language materials--Juvenile literature.] I. Bullock, Jungmiwha. II. Title.

PZ10.5.173.R33 BU   2014   401.93 [Fic]--dc22   2014906529

Printed in Canada
Smyth-sewn reinforced binding

Text type set in Calibri and KG fonts. Cover design and layout by Dr. Jungmiwha Bullock and Christopher Matthews. Select artwork donated and contributed by artist, Marquis Lewis, on classroom wall, playground scene floor, and Nicole's art canvas.

A Note on Understanding How to Read, *Am I Half Giraffe?*

FLAG MARKERS: Each of the translated languages herein is designated by a different country flag to only serve as a visual marker, making it easier for children to find their place with each turn of the page. We fully understand that many countries speak these same languages, and subsequently, could be represented by several flags simultaneously. Such flags are therefore represented in the other bilingual e-book versions of *Am I Half Giraffe?*, including languages not reflected in this multilingual edition.

TRANSLATIONS: The author translated and consulted with over 20 educators and professionals from around the world to ensure the cross-cultural meaning and multilingual accuracy of the story is universally understood across regions, no matter where each language is spoken. The main purpose of the translations is to inspire language literacy in children for years to come.

TEACHING TOOLS: We invite children, parents, educators, and librarians to use our downloadable teaching tools, which were created to accompany this unique book. The tools encourage readers to creatively explore and further discuss topics in this story, such as, friendship, family, bullying, identity, and more. Reading and learning languages is fun, but also requires continuous practice. Download activity worksheets, parent and teacher guides, and tutorials at: www.amihalfgiraffe.com.

KOREAN ALPHABET: The Korean and English alphabets are similar in pronunciation because both languages are phonetic. Whereas the English alphabet consists of 26 letters, the Korean alphabet includes 24 characters. Once you learn the characters and format of the Korean alphabet and their corresponding pronunciation, it is quite fun and easy to read. Visit our website for helpful resources to get you started.

AM I HALF GIRAFFE?

A Multilingual Book for Children

Dr. Jungmiwha Bullock
Illustrated by Christopher Matthews

HAPPY GROWING...

LEXIQUE DU MONDE
press

Washington, DC

« Chut, chuuut ! La voilà ! Regardez-la toute le monde ! »

C'est ce qu'ils disent à chaque fois que j'entre dans la pièce. Jusqu'ici, je croyais qu'ils disaient ça parce que j'ai l'air d'une superstar. C'est vrai quoi, regardez-moi ! Je ressemble à une célèbre actrice, non ?

"¡Shhh, shhhhh! ¡Ahí viene! ¡Miradla todos"!

Eso es lo que dicen cada vez que entro en el cuarto. Yo pensaba que era porque lucía como una súper estrella. Quiero decir, mírame, ¿no luzco como una actriz famosa?

"Shhh, shhhhh! Here she comes! Look at her everybody!"

That's what they say whenever I walk into the room. I used to think it was because I looked like a superstar. I mean, look at me, don't I look like a famous actress?

"쉬, 쉬~이! 걔가 온다! 모두 쟤 좀 봐!"

내가 교실에 들어갈 때마다 모두들 이 말을 한다. 나는 내가 슈퍼스타처럼 생겨서 그렇게 말한다고 생각하곤 했었다. 정말로 말이야. 나를 좀 봐, 연예인 같이 생기지 않았어?

"Shhh, shhhhh! Hier kom Sy! Kyk na haar, julle!"

Dis wat hulle sê wanneer ek by 'n vertrek instap. Ek het gedink dit was omdat ek soos 'n superster lyk. Ek bedoel, kyk na my, lyk ek nie soos 'n beroemde aktrise nie?

![French flag]

Malheureusement, ils me rappellent souvent que je ne suis pas du tout célèbre.

« Nicole, qu'est-ce qu'ils ont tes cheveux ? Les girafes n'ont pas des cheveux comme ça ! »

Tout le monde est d'accord et rit de moi en pointant du doigt ma somptueuse crinière.

![Spanish flag]

Desafortunadamente, a menudo me recuerdan que no soy tan famosa en absoluto.

"Nicole, ¿qué le pasa a tu cabello? ¡Las jirafas no tienen ese tipo de cabello"!

Todos están de acuerdo, mientras señalan y se ríen de mi melena llena de pelo.

Unfortunately, they often remind me that I am not so famous at all.

"Nicole, what's up with your hair? Giraffes don't have that kind of hair!"

Everyone agrees, while they all point and laugh at my full mane of hair.

그렇지만 걔네들은 내가 전혀 유명하지 않다는 것을 종종 상기시켜 준다.

"니콜, 너는 머리가 왜 그러니? 기린은 그런 머리를 가지고 있지 않아!"

모두가 동의한다. 내 풍성한 머리갈기를 보고 웃으면서.

Ongelukkig herinner hulle my dikwels daaraan dat ek glad nie so beroemd is nie.

"Nicole, wat gaan aan met jou hare? Kameelperde het nie sulke hare nie!"

Almal stem saam, terwyl hulle na my vol maanhare wys en lag.

« C'est parce que je suis moitié lion, moitié girafe. Ma crinière me vient de mon père, » dis-je fièrement.

« Mais tu n'as pas l'air d'être à moitié lion. Tu ressembles juste à une girafe mal coiffée ! »

Ils continuent de se moquer de moi.

"Eso es porque soy mitad león y mitad jirafa. Mi melena viene por parte de mi papá", les contesto con orgullo.

"Pero no pareces ser mitad león. ¡Solo pareces una jirafa con el cabello hecho un desastre"!

Todos se ríen de mí otra vez.

"That's because I'm half lion and half giraffe. My mane is from my dad's side," I say proudly.

"But, you don't look half lion. You just look like a giraffe with a bad hair day!"

They all laugh at me again.

그건 내가 사자 아빠하고 기린 엄마 사이에 태어나서 그래. "내 갈기는 아빠한테서 온 거야," 라고 난 자랑스럽게 말한다.

"하지만 넌 반쪽 사자 같지도 않아. 그냥 머리가 헝클어진 기린 같아!"

라고 내 기린 친구들은 다시 나를 비웃는다.

"Dis omdat ek half leeu en half kameelperd is. My maanhare kom van my pa se kant af," sê ek trots.

"Maar jy lyk nie half leeu nie. Jy lyk net soos 'n kameelperd met 'n slegte-haar dag."

Dan lag hulle almal weer vir my.

Je décide de les ignorer, comme je le fais toujours, mais à l'intérieur, j'ai mal. Ça fait vraiment mal.

Decido ignorarlos como siempre hago, pero en el fondo duele. Realmente duele.

I decide to ignore them like I always do, but deep down it hurts. It really hurts.

나는 늘 하는 것처럼 개들을 무시하기로 하지만 마음 깊숙이 상처가 된다. 정말 아프다.

Ek besluit om hulle te ignoreer soos ek maar altyd doen, maar diep binne maak dit seer. Dit maak regtig seer.

Vous savez, ce n'est pas la première fois que les girafes se moquent de moi à l'école. Oh, et il n'y a pas que mes amies girafes qui se moquent ! Mes amis lions le font aussi ! Comme aujourd'hui, même s'ils ne voulaient pas blesser mes sentiments, ça m'a quand même fait mal.

« Non, c'est toi qui demande. »
« Non, c'est toi qui voulais savoir, alors c'est toi qui demande. »
« Bon d'accord, j'y vais. »

Verás, esta no es la primera vez que las jirafas se burlan de mí en la escuela. Ah, y no son sólo mis amigas jirafas quienes lo hacen, mis amigos leones también se burlan. Como hoy, incluso cuando no pretenden herir mis sentimientos, de alguna forma sigue doliendo igualmente.

"No, pregúntale tú a ella".
"No, tú querías saberlo, así que tú pregúntale".
"Bien, iyo lo haré"!

You see, this isn't the first time the giraffes have made fun of me at school. Oh, and it's not just my giraffe friends who do it, my lion friends do it too. Like today, even when they didn't mean to hurt my feelings, somehow it still hurt anyway.

"No you ask her."
"No, you wanted to know, so you ask her."
"Okay fine, I'll do it!"

알다시피 학교에서 기린들이 나를 가지고 놀린 건 처음이 아니다. 아, 그리고 내 기린 친구들뿐만 아니라 내 사자 친구들도 똑같다. 오늘 같이 내 마음을 상하게 하려고 한 건 아니지만, 그래도 마음이 아프다.

"아니야, 네가 물어봐."
"아니, 네가 알고 싶어했으니까 네가 물어봐."
"좋아, 그렇게 할께!"

Julle sien, dit is nie die eerste keer dat kameelperde my by die skool spot nie. O, en dis nie net my kameelperd-vriende wat dit doen nie, my leeu-vriende maak ook so. Soos vandag, alhoewel hulle nie bedoel het om my gevoelens seer te maak nie, het dit nog maar steeds seergekry.

"Nee, vra jy vir haar."
"Nee, jy wou weet, so vra jy vir haar."
"Okay dan, ek sal dit doen."

« Hé Nicole, euh, donc... hum ... on se demandait tous... d'où viennent toutes ces taches rondes et claires ? Nous n'avons encore jamais vu un lion avec des taches pareilles. »

"Oye Nicole, eh, es que... bueno... todos estábamos pensando... ¿de dónde vienen todas esas manchas redondas claritas? Nunca habíamos visto a un león que las tuviera".

"Hey Nicole, uh, so... um... we were all wondering... where do all those light round spots come from? We've never seen a lion with them before."

"안녕 니콜, 근데... 근데... 우리 궁금한게 있는데... 그 둥근 반점들은 다 어디서 온 거야? 사자한테선 그런 걸 본적이 없는데."

"Haai Nicole, uh, so... um... ons wonder almal... waar kom al daardie ligte ronde kolle vandaan? Ons het nog nooit vantevore 'n leeu met sulkes gesien nie."

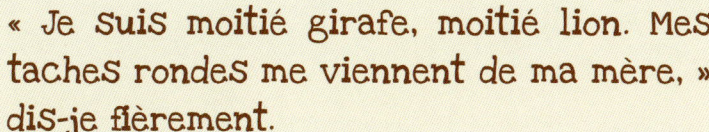

« Je suis moitié girafe, moitié lion. Mes taches rondes me viennent de ma mère, » dis-je fièrement.

« Mais tu n'as pas l'air d'être à moitié girafe. Ce serait mieux si tu n'avais pas toutes ces taches, non ? Tu serais plus comme nous ! »

Tout le monde me fixe en souriant, ils attendent que je les approuve.

"Soy mitad jirafa, mitad león. Mis manchas redondas vienen por parte de mi mamá", les contesto con orgullo.

"Pero no pareces mitad jirafa. ¿Alguna vez has deseado no tener esas manchas para parecerte más a nosotros"?

Todos sonríen y me miran, esperando a que yo esté de acuerdo.

"I am half giraffe, half lion. My spots are from my mom's side," I say proudly.

"But, you don't look half giraffe. Don't you ever wish you didn't have all those spots so you could look more like us?"

They all smile and stare at me, waiting for me to agree.

"나는 기린 반, 사자 반 이거든. 내 반점들은 엄마한테 물려받은 거야," 나는 자랑스럽게 말한다.

"그런데 너는 반도 기린처럼 보이지 않잖아. 너는 한번도 그런 반점들 없이 우리같이 보이고 싶기를 바란 적은 없니?" 걔들은 모두 웃으면서 나를 본다, 내가 동의하기를 기다리며.

걔들은 모두 웃으면서 나를 본다. 내가 동의하기를 기다리며.

"Ek is half kameelperd, half leeu. My kolle kom van my ma se kant af," sê ek trots.

"Maar jy lyk nie half kameelperd nie. Wens jy nie dat jy nie kolle gehad het, sodat jy meer soos ons kon lyk nie?"

Hulle wag vir my om saam te stem, terwyl hulle met 'n glimlag my aanstaar.

Je décide de les ignorer, comme je le fais toujours, mais à l'intérieur, j'ai mal. Ça fait vraiment mal.

Decido ignorarlos como siempre hago, pero en el fondo duele. Realmente duele.

I decide to ignore them like I always do, but deep down it hurts. It really hurts.

나는 늘 하는 것처럼 개들을 무시하기로 하지만 마음 깊숙이 상처가 된다. 정말 아프다.

Ek besluit om hulle te ignoreer soos ek altyd maar doen, maar diep binne maak dit seer. Dit maak regtig seer.

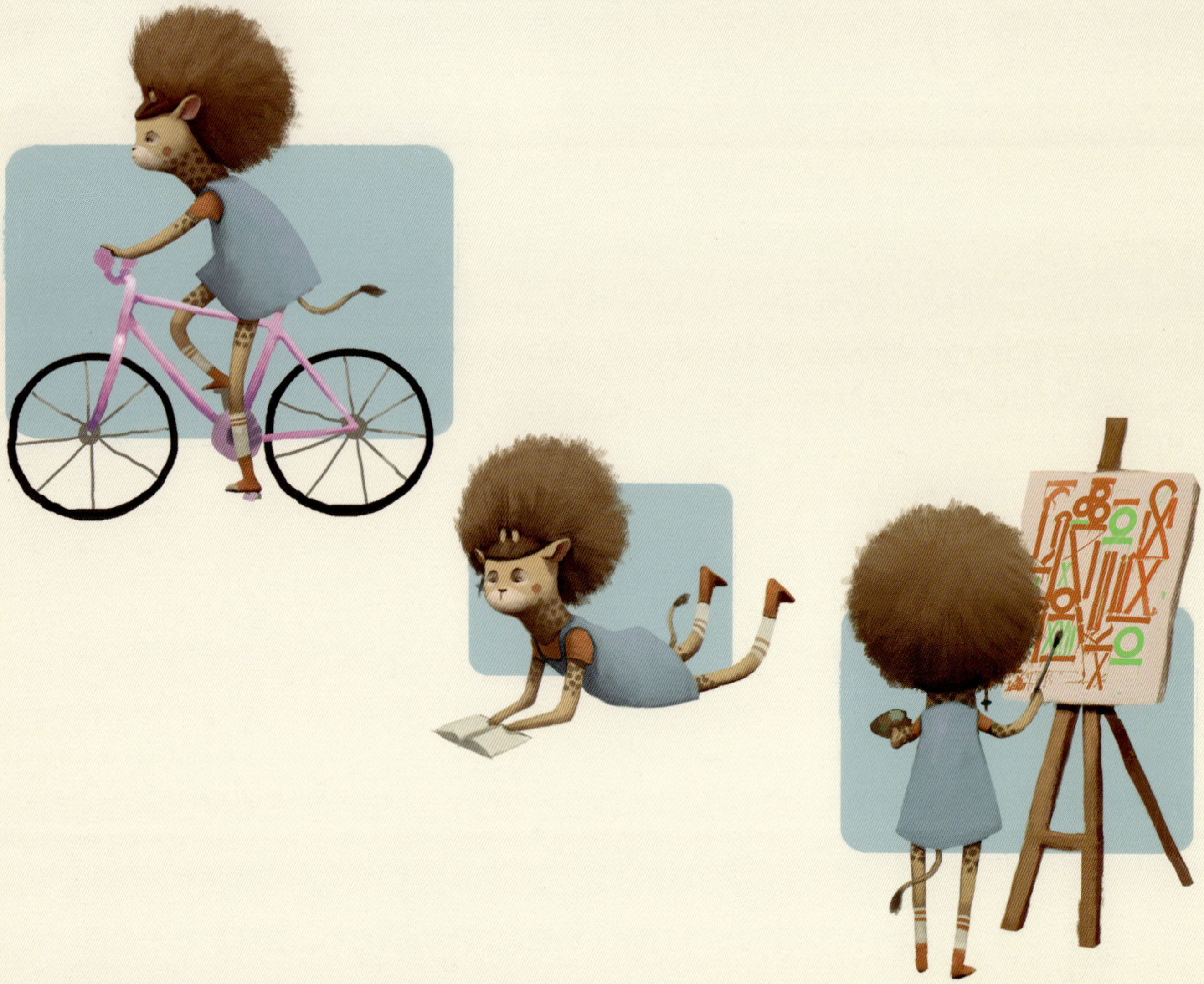

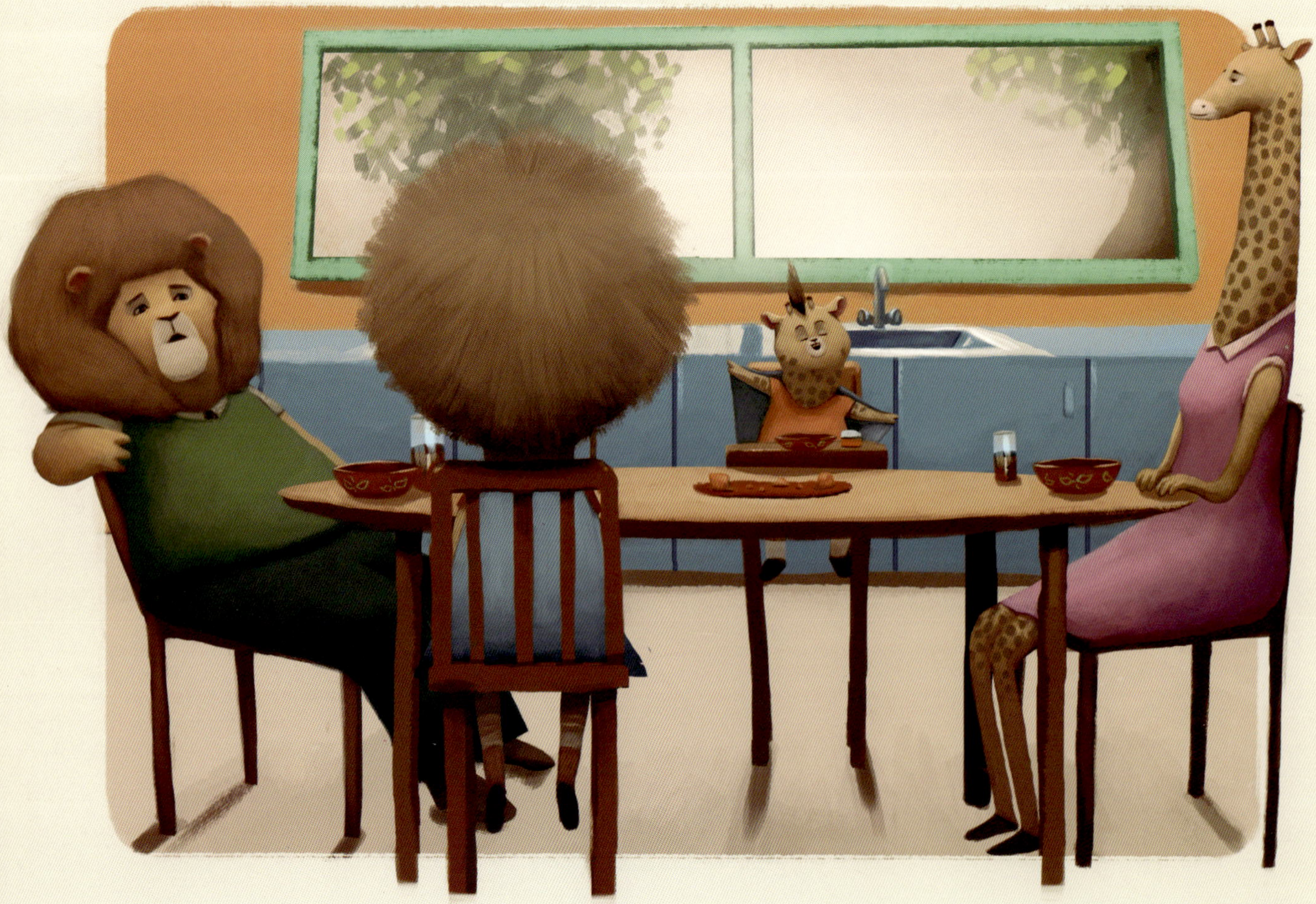

Le restant de la journée, je fais de mon mieux pour ne pas penser à tout ça. Du moins, jusqu'à l'heure du dîner.

« Maman, Papa, j'ai une question importante à vous poser. Je veux une réponse une bonne fois pour toutes. »

« Oui, Nicole, qu'est-ce qu'il y a ? » demande mon père.

Hago lo que puedo para no pensar en ello durante el resto del día. Bueno, al menos no hasta la hora de cenar.

"Mamá y Papá, tengo una pregunta muy importante que hacer. Debería ser contestada de una vez y por todas".

"Sí Nicole, ¿qué pasa?", preguntó mi papá.

I try my best not to think about it for the rest of the day. Well, at least not until dinner time.

"Mom and Dad, I have an important question to ask. It must be answered once and for all."

"Yes Nicole, what is it?" asked my dad.

나는 오늘 내내 그 일을 생각하지 않으려고 최선을 다한다, 적어도 저녁 먹을 때까진.

"엄마, 아빠, 나 중요한 질문을 하나 물어볼게 있어요. 꼭 한번에 모두 다 대답해 주셔야 해요."

"그래 니콜, 뭔데?" 아빠가 물어봤다.

Ek probeer my bes om die res van die dag nie daaraan te dink nie. Wel, ten minste nie tot aandete nie.

"Ma en Pa, ek het ŉ belangrike vraag om te vra. Dit moet eens en vir altyd beantwoord word."

"Ja Nicole, wat skort?" vra my pa.

« Suis-je moitié girafe ou moitié lion ? J'ai besoin de savoir. »

« Pourquoi demandes-tu cela, Nicole ? Tu es à la fois girafe *et* lion, » dit ma maman.

"¿Soy mitad jirafa o soy mitad león? Necesito saberlo".

"¿Qué te hace preguntar eso, Nicole? Eres tanto jirafa *y* león", dijo mi mamá.

"Am I half giraffe, or am I half lion? I need to know."

"What makes you ask that Nicole? You are both giraffe *and* lion," said my mom.

"나는 반쪽 기린인가요? 아니면 반쪽 사자인가요? 알아야 해요."

"니콜, 왜 그런 질문을 하는 거니? 너는 기린이고 또한 사자야," 엄마가 대답했다.

"Is ek half kameelperd, of is ek half leeu? Ek moet weet."

"Wat laat jou dit vra, Nicole? Jy is beide kameelperd *en* leeu," sê my ma.

« Je sais, mais pourquoi mes cheveux ne ressemblent pas à ceux des autres girafes ? Pourquoi les lions n'ont pas de taches comme les miennes ? »

Et c'est là que j'ai compris !

"Yo sé, pero, ¿por qué mi cabello no es como el de otras jirafas? ¿Por qué los leones no tienen manchas como las mías"?

¡Y en ese momento entendí!

"I know, but why does my hair not look like other giraffes? Why don't lions have spots like mine?"

And that's when it hit me!

"알아요, 하지만 왜 제 머리는 다른 기린과 다른 거죠? 왜 사자는 저처럼 둥근 반점이 없는 거죠?"

그때 비로소 난 깨닫는다!

"Ek weet, maar waarom lyk my hare nie soos ander kameelperde s'n nie? Waarom het leeus nie kolle soos myne nie?"

En dis toe dat dit tot my deurdring!

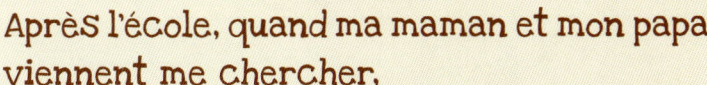

Après l'école, quand ma maman et mon papa viennent me chercher,

... et quand nous allons au jardin d'enfant récupérer mon petit frère,

... et quand nous prenons la voiture pour aller jusqu'au supermarché,

... et puis quand nous rentrons à la maison pour préparer le dîner ensemble, c'est évident. Vous savez...

Después de la escuela, cuando mi mamá y mi papá me recogen,

... y cuando vamos a la guardería a recoger a mi hermanito,

... y cuando conducimos hasta el mercado,

... y luego cuando volvemos a casa a preparar la cena juntos, es obvio. Verás...

After school when my mom and dad pick me up,

... and when we head to the daycare to pick up my little brother,

... and when we drive to the grocery store,

... and then head home to make dinner together, it is obvious. You see...

학교 수업 후에 엄마와 아빠가 나를 데리러 올 때,

... 그리고 남동생을 데리러 유치원에 갈 때,

... 그리고 마트에 장보러 갈 때,

... 그리고 저녁을 먹기 위해 집으로 갈 때, 당연한 건데.

봐...

Na skool, wanneer my ma en my pa my kom haal,

... en wanneer ons na die dagsorg gaan om my kleinboetie te gaan haal,

... en wanneer ons na die kruidenierswinkel toe ry,

... en dan huis toe gaan om saam aandete voor te berei, word dit duidelik. Julle sien...

Je ne suis pas juste moitié girafe.

No soy sólo mitad jirafa.

I am not just half giraffe.

 나는 그냥 반쪽 기린이 아니야.

 Ek is nie net half kameelperd nie.

Je ne suis pas juste moitié lion.

No soy sólo mitad león.

I am not just half lion.

나는 그냥 반쪽 사자가 아니야.

Ek is nie net half leeu nie.

Je suis tout ça... moi, Nicole.

Yo Soy enteramente... Nicole.

I am a whole... Nicole.

나는 온전해... 니콜.

Ek is 'n hele... Nicole.

To learn more about *Am I Half Giraffe?*, to read the author's note, and to access additional learning tools and resources, please visit:

www.amihalfgiraffe.com